בס"ד
לד' הארץ ומלואה

This book belongs to:

Please read it to me!

# The Creation Book

*To Yisroel & Esty, Naami & Yanky, Moshe & Eliana, Eli & Esther Malka, with love and gratitude.  D. A.*

First Edition – Elul 5778 / August 2018

Copyright © 2018 by HACHAI PUBLISHING
ALL RIGHTS RESERVED

Editor: D.L. Rosenfeld
Managing Editor: Yossi Leverton
Art Direction: Marc Lumer
Layout: Moshe Cohen

ISBN: 978-1-945560-06-4
LCCN: 2017953733

HACHAI PUBLISHING
Brooklyn, New York
Tel: 718-633-0100 • Fax: 718-633-0103
www.hachai.com • info@hachai.com

Printed in China

---

Glossary
Chava - Eve
Hashem - G-d
Shabbos Kodesh - Holy Sabbath

The illustration of Adam and Chava is for educational purposes and not meant to depict their actual appearance.

# THE CREATION BOOK

by Chani Gansburg
illustrated by Dena Ackerman

Black and white.
Dark and light.

Hashem made day.
Hashem made night.

He looked and saw

# Day 1

was done,
and it was good.

Crashing waves, rushing past.

Splashing rivers, flowing fast.

Brown and green, a bud, a bean.

Grass and fruit,

a rose,

a root.

On Day 3, Hashem made seas, sand and soil, plants and trees. Was it good? It was good.

Glowing **white,** the moon for **night.**

Stars and stars,
way up high
Planets spinning
in the sky.

On **Day 4,**
Hashem made lights
for the days
and for the nights.
And He saw that it was good.

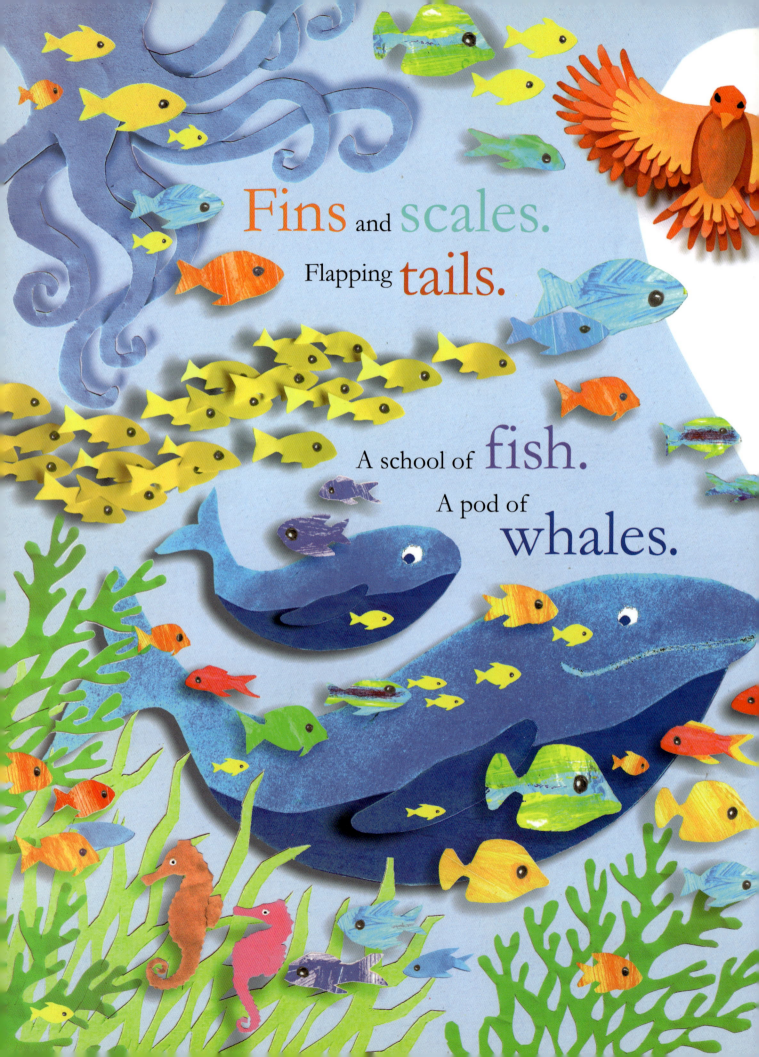

**Fins** and **scales.**
**Flapping tails.**

A school of **fish.**
A pod of **whales.**

A chirp. A quack.
A peck. A tweet.

Bills and beaks
and floppy feet.

Peacocks,
doves
and fluffy quails.

Leaping, creeping
frogs and snails.

On
Day 5,
things came alive.
Hashem filled
oceans and the sky
with things that squirm
and swim and fly.

And He saw that
it was good.

A set of hooves.
A foot. A paw.

To clip and clop.
To climb. To claw.

Silky manes, shiny fur.

Lions roar.
Tigers purr.

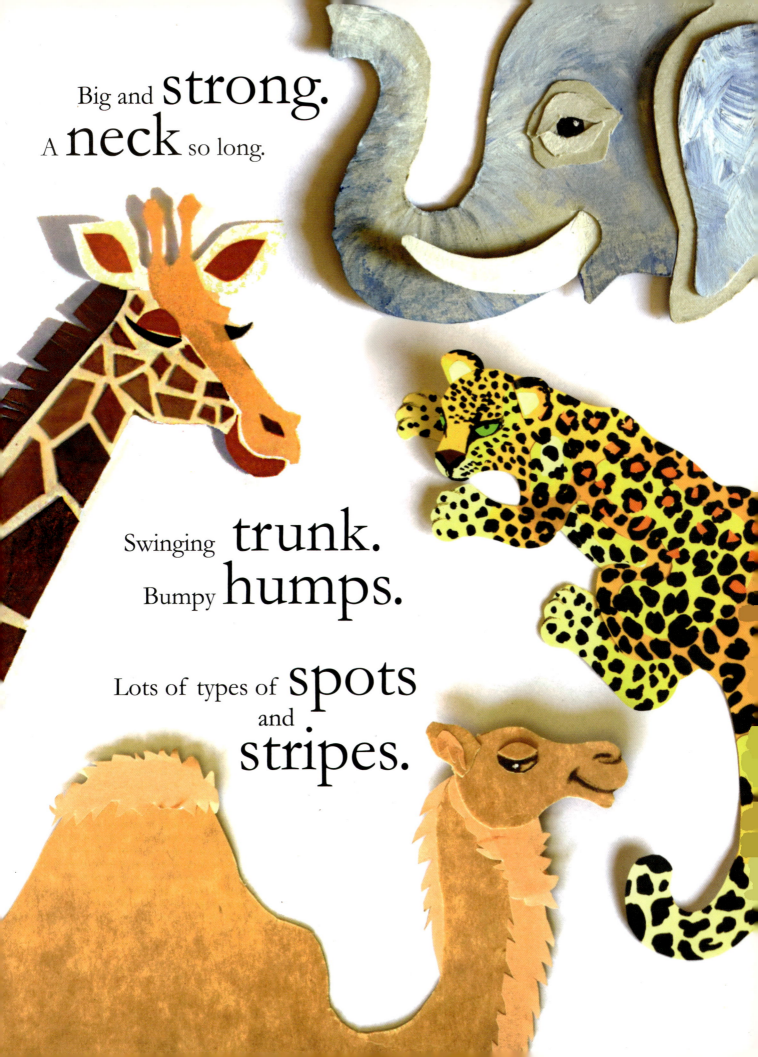

Big and strong.
A neck so long.

Swinging trunk.
Bumpy humps.

Lots of types of spots and stripes.

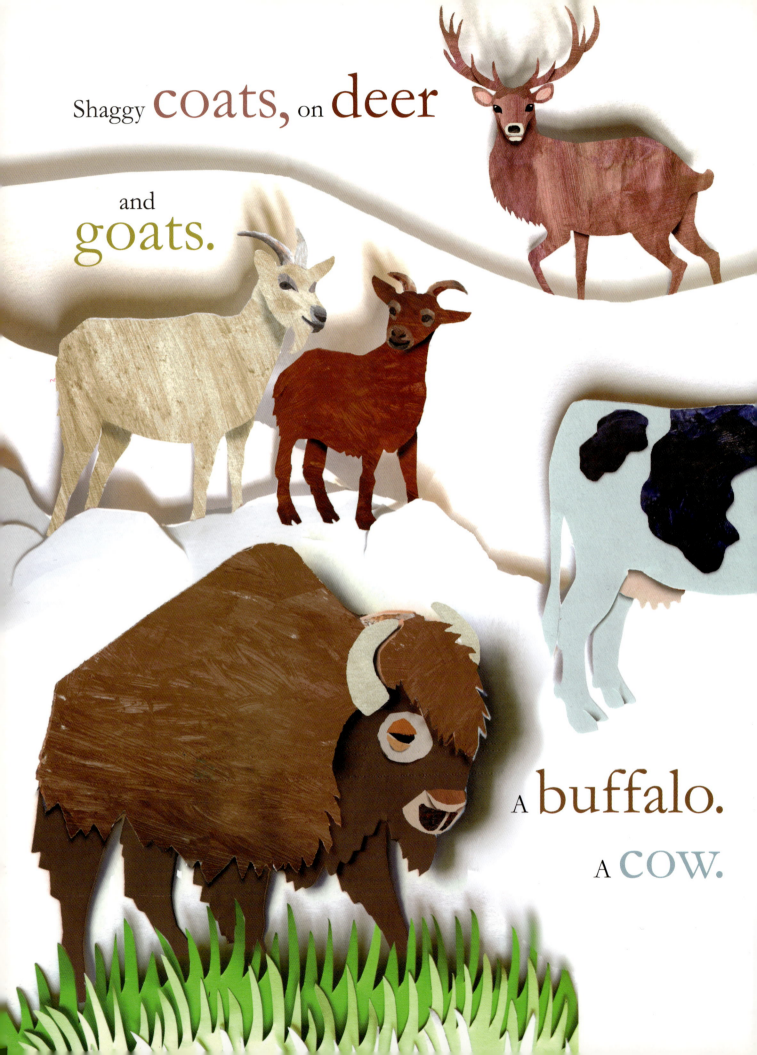

Shaggy coats, on deer and goats.

A buffalo. A cow.

A bull.

Rams for shofars.

Sheep for wool.

Animals with cud to chew.
And with hooves, each split in two.

And He saw that it was good.

The work of every day was done.

Six, five, four, three, two, and One.

Days with light and dark for night.

Seas in place, a sky in space.

Hills all slanted, trees all planted.

Stones all shaped, vines all draped.

The sun and moon
and stars so high.

Fish that swish
and
birds that fly.

Animals that
roam the land.

Man and woman
made as planned.

One more
thing for
Hashem to make…

a day to stop, to take a break.

Day 7 is a day of rest.
Shabbos Kodesh we love best.

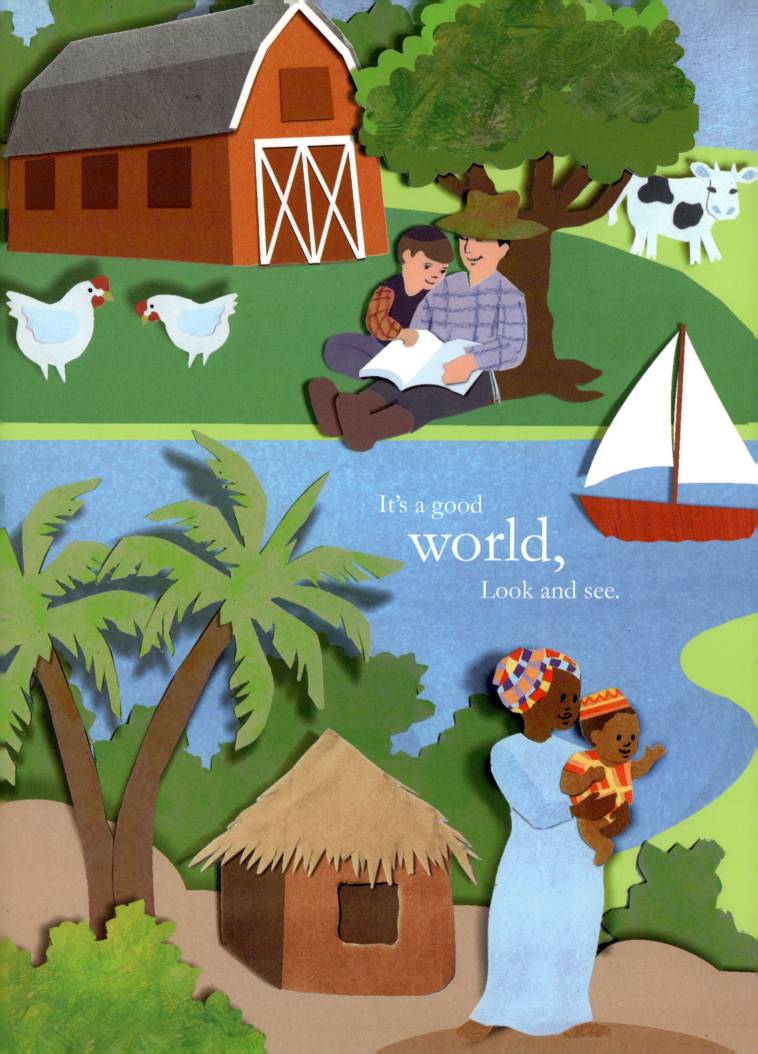

It's a good **world,**
Look and see.

Made by Hashem, for **you** and **me.**